carved.

collected poems
by bbezra

copyright @2021 bbezra
all rights reserved
illustrations & cover via Canva

*for my mother
who always listened
and in doing so
left an indelible mark
on my words.*

the poems.

When I started to 'whittle' down this collection, I noted that I have been writing often about breath, love and death as themes.
I think that's because those words and realities are shaping my life right now.
small repeated movements, precise.
Carving the shape of my moments.
When I stepped back
-to trace the formed intricacies-
I saw another theme emerge.
Home.
A home in my flesh, not one for it.
Yes, the process may be painful, but the result is beautiful.
I hope you will enjoy these poems, that one or two might serve as a small chisel as you form
your own edifice to living.
I would consider myself fortunate indeed if perhaps they might leave a small pattern,
something ornate and lovely on your soul.
-bbezra

carved

Carved.
i sit.   wooden flesh   &stone
ponder…
Carved.
whittled. sliced . hewn.
the nature of carved
the structural nature
of inflicted damage
purposeful or no…
Scarred.
irrefutable lineage.
of pain. or change.
cutting. carved.
(bruises) heal
wounds.   always.
leave. a trace
cellular…. dna
seen.   surfaced.
a tree
may grow around the
puncture
layered ring upon ring
but in death & deeper cutting
it.   is clearly seen.

Carved.
Visible.
shaped stone stays
as.   shaped
owning the form   imparted
by chisel.   by blade.
only ever dissipates….
migrating form into dust
i suppose the same
is true of us.
Carved.
i too.   wooden flesh.   & stone.
wonder…
Carved.
artifice.   artifact.   art.
or just bonded.   to the past
in   inescapable
patterns on my skin.

wood.

1.

i am not so easy
to love
to find in
un- guarded moments
peppermint
& shaded
thicket'd
tree lines
i am not so
easy.　love.　to find
tucked away
lily of the valley
early spring sonnet
&
dandelion
(on)　　summer's final breeze
there is no ease
love me if you love me
autumnally.
love me in deaths
&dying
blooming & remembering
-love.

i sway
i am not fixed
& do not stay
ever changing course
ever moved
i am all toss'd
& fade & dance in fragrant meadow
no.
i am not so easy
to love.

2.

meet me.   my love
by… the trumpet-vine
where… it winds (full of blossom)
Breathe
softly with me
by… its rambled leaf
and… underneath
its   fragrant dome
brush. past.   my lips
(with)   rapt   eagerness
stealing. bliss.   (from moments)
meant for hummingbirds alone

3.

&
you taught me
sweetness
dripping.
down my chin
mouthfuls
of flesh
only
ever.   met by sunshine
& sweet rain
you.
taught me unfiltered bliss
innocence borne
After.   knowledge
a garden of eden
After.
the world fell
to darkness
& hopelessness
your.   theology redeemed me
your form.   your <u>features</u>
your.   words spilling from those <u>perfect lips</u>
a divine mandate
taste
& believe again
that
there is still goodness in earth
and   sky
& breath.

4.

i like things
that.   feel
Ancient
& early & wise
mountains
with moss'd stone
    and your Sunday
eyes...

i like
laughter
that.   rings out
down empty. back. stairs.
echoes
'round corners
reverberates
there...

i like moments
when heartache's
    12 miles away
somewhere.
still distant
arrival delayed....

i like things
that.   are
Hopeful
& new & surprised
sunrise
in fresh sheets
and.   your Sunday eyes...

5.

when. i am tired. & small
(like i am today)
when.   the expanse of
my internal
structured. organized. thrice folded towel linen cupboard life
has. become   (itself)
compressed & splintered
-fragmented
then.   i reach inside
(grasp the slender thread)
silver gossamer   that.   still ties me to this. world
i follow it down
to my core
bleeding
as i go
torn.   by.   shards
i have carefully sorted
-wrapped cotton gauze
-in layers
-hidden from prying eyes
& disapproving aunties
until.   i reach
there. *the core.*
the. unraveling. place.
(where)

i pause

& contemplate in silence
& distant sobbing &
someone's dissonant laughter
the simplicity of fabric
(so easy)
to.
snip. this.   slip of silk…
instead.
i force myself to touch
the softness.
feel it supple & yielded
&*vulnerable* between thumb   & finger
fine. Woven.

i gather it up
(as much as can fill my arms)
& wrap myself around
it. tender gift of spun time
(sharp edges & all)
i.   bury my face   & sing about
Tomorrow.

6.

(evening prayers)
then.
sepia'd afternoon… burdened haze & warmth
sighed with relief at daylight's fading strength
an exhaled breeze that began atop
tall trees & cyclone'd down
&*round* & round

caught our hair
our skin
we.   drenched in exertion…
had traveled too far.
gone miles beyond our stopping point.

you paused.   to gulp the
vesper'd sweetness
tasting momentary release from
heat & destination

when
one lingering shy gaze (through closing twilight's veil)
traced your form
eyes, shoulders, neck then lips
envisioned souls, intertwined & soft
a pair, *belonging*
&longing &longing

rhythm of
footfalls
heavier on stone than soil
echoed along
sandy curves & wind bent leaves

do you remember what you shared with me?

as darkness
swallowed up restraint
you *inked* night things you had to say
& i your temporary parchment...

tumbling careless truths sacred hopes
wandering hungers cloaked beliefs
that were not mine to hear, I knew. & knew & *knew*

those words
said not for me.   confessed beneath dim stars.
borrowed.   intimate.   liturgy.
i its acolyte
(carry still the pain of substitution)
& your silence as you turned to go
in emptied.   absolution.

7.

i thought.　　death was something somber
a door
ornate & heavy.　　　made
from.　an ancient tree
wood. Hewn.　　still alive
this.　the portal from one dimensional
reality to the next
i. had thought.　　greeting it with a sober
mind.　a pensive heart
the correct approach
(after all).　　every ending
deserves the weight
of its own propriety　　& finality.

i have learned.　　death is something　　*else* entirely
-a beaded curtain
strung.　haphazardly
more　　　　suggestion
than boundary line
-a blurred screen
-a muted view
into.　one room over

where people you.　　haven't met yet
are watching reruns.
a show everyone has seen
but cannot remember.

8.

i went.
to visit you today
the halls smelled   of cleaning solution
i followed the flicker
of   fluorescent lights
through the maze of scrub-bedecked
attendants
to a row of uncomfortable. chairs.
near a vending machine
waiting my turn
to hold your hand and say
'i love you'
over the hiss of oxygen
& my own tears.

i went.
to visit you today
the earth smelled   of growing grass
i followed the winding
stone. path.
through a maze of other people's
sorrows
near a massive oak tree
attending
to the granite stone   that tells the world
you belonged to someone.
taking my turn to hold flowers
& whisper
'i love you'
over the song of birds
& nothing else.

9.

laid out. neatly. on the bed
dresses
gone unworn
stacked shoes
stilted stories
& whispered conversations
narrow hallways
locked doors.　　opened
intrusion
did she miss　the marketplace
a paper's space　between
Illusions
Confusion.　squared.
Rapt　ever　wrapped　ever
Bound ever
by a prayer
Prayer to the rooftops
& steeples
Above a　sky
cerulean mingled with honeysuckle
bees repeating the same song
to each other
all this
On a day that should have been brighter
she.　tore the dress
& laid the rest.　to rest.

10.

do you really think
i don't see it
the combined hesitancy
& tender pity in your gaze?

after what you know of
me...you don't think i can see
the packed bags in the hall?

i knew.
from the first moment you
stood on my doorstep
hat in hand
gently smiling...

i knew

i saw the end.
at the beginning.
saw the whole thing.
darling.

don't pity me for choosing
you anyway.
when i   knew you
couldn't stay.
the moments between
your arrival

& your departure

are worth the inevitable.

11.

he/him
(a poltergeist)
a smithy.
a.　　shell. where a threadbare.　　soul
padded　　　about. on.　threadbare
carpet. in a room with no heat.
smoked another
cigarette…
considered they/them (him).
habitual.　this.　practice.
of segmenting.　an utter nothingness
casting
& returning empty
of stones.　　& supper.　　and joy.
layered upon layer
peeling wallpaper.　something hung
placed with purpose & paste
by. someone.
someone. else…

                    they/themselves
                  (poltergeist) an entity
        a.   hell. for a threadbare soul.
                padding himself in threadbare
                        philosophies...
                    bleeding through
                   nicotine.   stains.
                 imbedded in the swirls
                    on a fingertip
                   residue this tobacco'd.
                   version of absolutes.
                   a thousand
        washes in a sink.   a rusty spigot.
         piped production of shudder
                      & scream
                   never.   clean.
                 faded echoes.
                       former.   lives.
        simplistically calls us liars.
                        all.   us/we
                  labeled superficiality.
                spiders in.   corners
        unused dustpans.   an. oven
                 with a broken door
                    &   he/him.
                       chained.
              haunting imposed banality.
                        hid there
        between dopamine & self loathing
                    self soothing.
              in.   smoke rings
                       an unfettered truth...
                 even his own cherished
        honesty.   Isn't real.

12.

i.   think today
perhaps.
i am not.   a tree
rather
something.   older still
i am the soil   roots wrap
themselves in.
loamy
dark. damp.
my. own earthen self
made of
green & rot
what has come.   before
i live
hidden from the.   blue of sky
ever- indifferent to the
song of birds

13.

tender whisper
i do not trust
hushed sincerity
resonance of breath & lip
for me alone to hear
sotto confessions
pianissimo passion
no word it's singularity
vows spoken in such subtlety
(claimant without guarantee)
i have heard before...
still.　　i long for tempered tones
dulcet
lies for me alone
soft pressed
& near
　　　　my cheek
my ear
a paradise　　in listening.

14.

     my description of
         warm earth

  &   hot sun
    fell short
        of that day
in the meadow
when you held my hand
and the world felt
   planted anew.

15.

i. will not softly.　weep
& grieve the parting
of this passion
a dirge unsung
in notated sigh.
rhythm'd beats
have driven me
from bustling streets
glistening with brick
& rain
those fair fat souls
that bread sustains
led me...
to the catacombs
beneath
i'll follow echos
find. you there
my. hidden.　heart
my latent smile
my languid hope
laid dormant
under stone & steel
One breath
One thought
One kiss.
& then to ever-bearing life
& dust then
hope
& dust again

16.

i.
have poured out
oceans

seas.
rivers.
tributaries of my soul

a rapid vortex'd outflow
depths of glacial undertow

for you.

you…plastic soul that you are.

have taken everything

fresh. flowing.
sweetly life sustaining

& bottled it

17.

a love poem?
not today. not in this
day fraught with small
delights…
i will not blight this
sunlight. this laughter.
your shoulder upon
my own with
a love poem…
instead.   i will
breathe & be
grateful
that on this …most
ordinary
of days, i have met
common eternity
wearing
wind rustled leaves
& the crinkled
corners of
your eyes.

18.

what sort of soul are you?

inked. ever. in the ether
of surrealist dreams
a hazy form from Misted
forests
a soft step at dawn upon
fragrant carpet
fringed in clover

what soul are You?

seen. ever. in fragments
shadowed pieces

a stippLed impression
moments
a spun secret of refracted dew
an intricate web
pained by beauty

what sort Of soul are you?

whose thought comes
unbidden
footfalls upon
my silent meadow'd
contemplation
you.
sweetest. Variable
Encompassing intrusion

what soul. are you?

19.

i would. burn it all down
for.   five minutes with you
i'd.   throw it all away. trash.   Accolades.
tear up borrowed. truth.
set it ablaze.
knowing your gaze
is all I need know
i.   would light flame walk
in epic slow mo
let what is behind me behind me
simply explode.
my storehouse of knowledge
a
kindling (as such)
in this bonfire stoked
there is nothing I will not watch
combust.   for this truth.
the ending. to wanting.
the beginning. of having.
the phosphorus heat latent between us two.
yes darling. ashes scattered around
i'd burn it all down for.   five minutes
with you.

20.

verbal bracken
words 'round my neck &
can't catch my breath.

i know it's a lie
that you'll love me til death

& it's one that I want to
Believe.

cistern'd well emotion
eloquent fool's portion
can't keep my head.

i know you're a book
that I shouldn't have read

& you're one that I still want to
Read.

an undoing
(let's have one)
a spell breaking
(it's become one)...

i'd like to say love won

but it's just not the truth.

21.

Oh! to find home.

the tongue cannot
  regain the taste of
cardamom & mint

  nor.   feet the
      stomp & sway
of joyful dance

if lips never part
to taste. again.

if music never
finds your soul. again.

(do not hide a life in
    rented niceties…
        devoid of truth)
  spice.
it must be crushed —my love
  fragrant & layered
  to impart flavor

rhythm.
it finds its way — my love
paths of sound & emotion
villages of flesh

place. owned. known.

& this…

this. growing wildness
whispered on the wind
'go…feel again'
that.
is a homeland too.

22.

Today. to cope with the pain
i am -not- sitting down
i   am opening blinds
i.   am wiping down walls
(in case there's any trace of you
in a corner I forgot to dust)
.   to cope with the pain
i am tending to things
i've forgotten
just. me.   Alone
sharpening kitchen. knives
oiling. bamboo cutting boards
sorting through
old Christmas cards
(trying not to think about all the
ways you smiled
and why that's painful right now)
Today.   i am choosing to
find. myself.   Again.
in mundane tasks
that smell
Of orange oil
& cedar & clean floors
and hard fought
Peace.

23.

every.   time.   i reach for you
i pull back handfuls of solitude
fists. full.   of lonely
every.   time.   i call out for you
returned. echos from some
fathomless   abyss
(you).   never answer back

every.   time.   you reach for me
i. shift nearer   in eager. embrace.
every. time.   you call for me
i stand tenderly, listening
hands   gently on your face
you know…
i'm here….
(because)
i am always here….painfully.
foolishly.   willingly.   here.
every.   time.

flesh & bone.

24.

Is it ok with you-society that worships youth-

if i age?

if i willingly allow the ravages of time to whisper lines across my face

if i trade

nights of youthful impudence for the rhythm of sunrise and sitting. if i age?

if i remit apology for allowing me to settle in
to nights infused with heat and comfort, to linger longer at a page, to drink too little, to forget.

to decide on purpose not to rage and reach for what is fleeting

to pursue this retreating of fresh bloom and lust and glow

and let myself go
be ok with this place

to age. beautifully, unpretentiously, defiantly

to embrace what makes you turn away.

25.

it. is. not.
my bones that are brittle.
they may well bear the
pressure of this
weight.

it. is. not.
my soul that is fragile.
it is resilient enough for the
sorrow of this
moment.

it. is. my.
poor heart
that sings hope
which has failed me
in this task of
staying strong enough.

26.

my bones wept today, at the approach of light
begged me to consider
keeping still
& laying longer
In the softness before dawn...
i hesitated.
convinced
by their testimony
i am too tired to rise...

Then

as if a herald
from
a moment yet to come
a thrush
at my window
greeted
the day impassioned.
in the melody of his warble
i anticipated.
convinced by his effervescence
i am
too alive
to sleep.

27.

un-named solace
earthen sacraments
in lazy afternoon
reveries
under.   sheets
& subtleties
dearest distraction
ever. saving. this fool
feasting on
apportioned sorrows
larder'd to nibble on
during….dark days
earnest.
soft brush of hand
against my own
leading. gently.   to
reaction & responding
sweetest lips
soft with life part
me in blissful.   surrender
sharing, stealing.   air.
whispering recollections.   of smiles
without a sigh.

28.

you voiced
your unmet
expectations
with your eyes,
& I had absolutely no response
except to justify my actions
with silent justification.

I said nothing
to your *everything*
met your pleading
with moralistic obligations
that left me feeling
<u>unfulfilled.</u>

ok.
So that's us now. -
Moments that fall short
of what either of us want

&
neither one is able
to reach beyond
those moments in the doorway
where we brush
past each other
like it's normal.

It's not normal.
no one here is normal.
If I have figured
anything out
—and I have not—
it's that.

so let's play
pretend again.
& again & again.

Please—
so we can get our
feet torn up on the eggshells;
or the
hot coals;
or whatever metaphor we are walking
around in right now.

this quiet battle of wills
is the loudest fight
We've ever had...
YOU WIN.

29.

Oh nascent anger!
Embryonic hope.
Gestated emotions,
un-birthed in time
the pain of offering
You breath
is as fruitless
as my womb.
(Miscarried)

30.

    bound.   & bonded
    settled accounts
      reconcile. them
  with small amounts
  hastened. hardship.
     burn the ends
   frayed. & withered
    played pretense.

That. nothing scars
That. nothing scars
That. nothing scars
    my skin.

   aged.   & aching
  nerves.   that scorch
 sharpened. breaking.
    furrowed earth
   time.   & tremors
   false made pure
  locked.   & losing
   grand. austere.

And. nothing stops
And. nothing stops
And. nothing stops
    the pain.

31.

take a lover
(take ten)
what have they to do
with you & i?
another's breath
a longing sigh...
am i so small as to

want you
simply.
for a hand to hold?
a mouth to press
against
in primal.　heat?
tell me darling-
what have your
lovers to do
with me?

give your temporary
flesh
to temporary
pursuits
borne of impermanent
seed & dying fruit

give your body
(as you will)
'tis a sarcophagus
of skin. & sinew
to thrust against
then to dust

offer me that instead
which does not fade
at early light
or waning lust
this. Infinite bond
connecting us
philosophies, eternities
thoughts that bind
give that which perishes
to the dying
give to me your soul
vow to me your mind.

32.

today…
with its tangled
conversations
missed moments
& unsung love songs…
lets us
wash it in
dusk
and softness

Permit early stars to
Remit that slight
Headache

heartache

mistakes.

tonight…
with its twilight
accommodations
sans reason
& reasoned wrongs
lets us
wash in it
night
and stillness.

a coverlet of yielded tranquility.
& stars.

33.

"Hesitation is
Regret come early"
She said to me
In a knowing tone
As she wiped her hands
On an apron
Nodding toward my own hands
-clenched now
tense
Each time the door swung open
Her eyes softened as she
Poured me more coffee
Positioning her frame
Between my table
& *that* door
She smiled and held
My gaze
"Since you have to wait"
She said
"Wait happy.
Have cream
Have sugar
This moment....."
She smoothed her uniform
"......Is yours
When it's the moment
You're dreading
You'll know what
To do."

34.

Do not write another poem
About love
Write instead
A meeting
Of surrendered minds
Reflecting
On the concourse of stars
Or the fragility
Of time
Not love
Not emotional
Drippy love
As if grasping and having
and owning and knowing
Are love at all
What foolish notions these ideas of love
Fraught with moments of rapture and delight
Love is not transcendence
Love is base
Love is Service to another's needs
And wants
Without a thought for your own

It is the unpopular notion
That goes Un-worshipped
Un-met in the alleyways of lust and passion
What We chart as love
True love real love
In its description would be tossed away
Defined as toxicity even abuse
because it's a continuous sacrifice
That allows infinite use
It is not simply unadorned beauty
That owns no accolades
It's weary sleepless nights spent
Covering another's shame
It is washing unwashed bodies
Who long ago surrendered
Themselves to recesses
Of consciousness or pain
Journeyed beyond what's reachable
Un-knowable. Un-teachable.
Love is daily *intentional* ministrations
Valueless to that one
That cannot offer
Loveliness or safety or reciprocity
or satisfaction
Or gratitude.
No.
Love is not a platitude.

35.

there are no words for her
this specter between us.. a phantom that has slowly
lost her rooted reality
& become a golden
Honey'd version
of a love you once held

36.

slice.
open my. skin.
with words… you don't mean
'i want you.'
'I'll be there'
'you're beautiful'…

i'll bleed
& you'll ignore it
pooling… on the floor
it's.
a momentary
Inconvenience
sorry. that you
had to see this.

yes, i'll clean it
Up.

'cause
i'd do anything
just to feel your
love.

37.

an eon ago
i was ancient
& young
& older still
days extended beyond sand
& stars
& tiny specks of sunlight freckling skin
then.
you appeared.
& wellsprings gave
their hoarded trove
& life began again
those wastelands that desire you?
my love…
if it brings you pleasure
in this reality
let them eat their fill
& sup.
leave for me only
at end of day
these bones
memorial feast to gnaw upon
on winters harsh
& cold
a gravestone I can vigil at
& remember
immortality

i have loved you
emptied.　for a thousand
generations
& will love you still
again
in leanness, in plenty
my desire is not met by
fat & meat
& marrow
simply leave
all
you've ever offered
…leave to me your bones

38.

          come.   to me soon
         (or send your ghost)
           a. phantom kiss
       to. drive shadows. under the bed
         to. have tea   with the monsters
            come.   to me soon
      brush your soul along the cracks in mine
           melding gold in every line
              teach.   me.
           your far flung ancient answers
                to beauty
               come. to me
       press.   your agonies over my own &
    let. them. move in tandem.   Rhythmic.   Cardiactic.
              Sorrow to sorrow
               palm on palm
         encompassing.   penetrating the
            recesses…. in divided reality
           come soon. come soon to me.
         whispers across portal'd dimension
         sotto past & present   portent of
                future.   solidarity
         welded.   spans of measured history
            layered.   infinite in filigree
             sweet.   line upon sweet. line
              ever undoing & renewing
                  time….
                do not delay
               come to me soon
                  my love
                  come to me

39.

i think perhaps.
i'd rather
not.
linger in your eyes
the possibility
there between your
iris & my soul
well- it's too much sight
& seeing
for me
i need to.
(run)
away.
from the home
offered in your
ocular tenderness.
not because i
daren't reflect
my own longing…
rather
i do not wish to see
the unabashed truth
beyond the brightness
of your returned gaze.
(one day)
soon. too soon
for my heart.

you.
Will
look past me
As well.

stone.

40.

i tried.
to stay in love
with you.
(i know you won't believe me)
& why should you?
after all…you never knew…
i fought. alone.
for love   in quiet moments
between solitary heartbeats
& bedsheets.
your warmth
at night…turned cold.   to me.
as i lay
breath by breath
felt love slip away.

i tried.
to stay in love
with you.
(i know that's what you needed)
can i need too?
after all…it does take two…
to find. a path through…
i wandered. unaccompanied.
the maze.   the myriad pains
within un-generous conversation
& change.
still…wanted to
live…in pleasant.   harmony.
as i ached
day by day
for real embrace.

i tried
to stay in love
with you.
(i know the answer already)
could you forgive me?
for all…the painful moments…
after this.　　it is not ill-intended.
despite.　　　my efforts to
(i made more than a few)
-more than i've said.
-more than you knew.
i worked. to stay.
i tried to stay

in love with you.
but i simply
am not
able to.

41.

i will.
follow this pattern
to.   its
verdant conclusion
the. wanting
sown deep.
in.   meaning
borne
deep in   longing
i will press.   my lips
in unformed phrases
along
trenched Truth
unexplored   equation.
foundation.
& ache for
(Satisfaction)
that cannot be.
will not be.   realized
without this.

                This.
         unbound desire
              loosened
  from.   the core of earth itself
          magma'd passion
           hot & heedless
            ever-shifting
          Teutonic plates
      creating.   continents
                slow
                ruin.
         (without apology)
             loam fertile
                with
        Released. possibilities
                child
           of fire & earth

it. was a gutted gravel road
…i remember that.
…i remember seeing
my childhood feet
clad. dirty white sandals just too big
making their their way along
one foot in front of the other
a balance beam
only… it was just me
& a narrow creek.
& some formless faces
Ambling down the road.
waves of heat
risen, undulating in the distance…
someone sang softly
songs i knew vaguely…

such a thing to remember
this.   one thing i so often
Remember. This. Vividly.
transported in grocery store
check out lines
Or.
right before i succumb to sleep

the history.
of a full life lived
smells.   of summer
sounds.   of voices
& one foot clumsily
in front of another
on a path i
cannot quite recall.

43.

time's herald
he that is but face
& formed
midwife'd
met upon
this fixed point

now.

arrival
day and dawn
exerts his span
upon

Fragile Mortality

Moments summoned
—not deeded nor
Defied

Temporary
Begets
Eternity.

44.

why am I swayed?
how is it that feet
this.
staunchly.
planted.
are so easily shifted...
am i that malleable?
i have forged a lifetime
-my lifetime
tempering emotions
to will
how then-
just the thought
of you...
not.
even a lingering thought.
a momentary
singular
innocent thought.
& fortitude crumbles
i'm so angry at my own heart!
turncoat to reason and mastery
these unquenched feelings
will be the end of me
how can I possibly cross the span
of mortal time
breathe each day
under this weight of wanting.

45.

proof my love?
an unnecessary
concept
measured in uncertainty
prove it. proof. proven.
what are these words to me?
do you wish actions
forged in flame
hammered.   ever.
under constant steady
tending?
can passion be so
proven?
dross in it enough. even.
to assuage your
doubt?
how to prove what is?
what. has. been.
ever. will. Be
(has never stopped)
(goes surrendered & un-surrendered)
proof.   my love
of…   our infinity?
all
things begin and
end in fire.

46.

maybe.
this soul is
too. weathered
this ground too.
Parched
for the seed
of your affection
i think
anything
that was alive and willing
to.
reach for warmth
& light
turned to dust.
just.
before you arrived.

47.

this. small stone
-Thrown
into a pool
of undetermined depth
disturbs clarity
impedes Reflect
a confluence of merged
Vicissitude
neither calmer for it
the aquifer or I...
both displaced.
One in turmoil
One at loss
'Careless toss'
this. small stone
-Thrown
torn from riparian cradle
solitary
Terra interloper
rippled waves
that form
&
stagnate
On ponded Skin
in
a singular impingement
this. small stone
-Thrown
Leaves
it's   mark

on me. Alone.

48.

am i
entombed
in this solitude?
have i
wrapped.
myself.   in swathes
& silences
believed them
to be
a gossamer
Chrysalis
when this.
un-ember'd cold
& comfort
& quiet is
a sepulcher?
(monument to all I didn't say)

49.

    wrap me in
   funerary clothes
    lead me veiled
      I care not for
violets underfoot i go
mourn my heart's travail.

they go in threes the
    grey dawn sang
   they go on winds
    of south and east
   they go away
     blacken brick
& hearts they go in threes.

      then.
    laid me
    on the
    upturned sod
   tell me tales
     un-beholden to
  life & death &
   faith in gods
love that 'ere prevails

they come in pairs
the North Star sang
they go in pairs
the turtle dove
they fly away
& talk of rain
& dreams they know not of

part me from the
lips I know
held my life
& hold it still
pale, devoid of joy or hope
left to worm and time.

they leave as one
the song remains
they leave as one
in solitude
they go alone
to soul & deep
lost to light & pulchritude

this ancient truth I bind in breath
as life is bound itself by death
& You leave mourned by me.

50.

go ahead.
say
(those) things we shouldn't say
my heart's been whispering them

Anyway.

51.

"There is poetry there"
I said to myself
Hair up
Saturday night
lavender bath
as steam wafted
I wrestled with
Wayward adjectives
&
spent illusions

Compelling
Syllable & love
into this interlude
write sonnets. ink reveries.
Odes to solitude

"There is poetry there"
I argued with myself
Fists out
Ready to fight
my demons who
(as night deepened)
Feasted on faint joy
Fattened indifference
&
small delusions

"There is poetry there"
(Perhaps.)
& yet, tonight
it goes unwritten.

This Silence will not relent.

52.

         perhaps.
we.   venerate the dead
         because
      they.   stay.
they.   cannot leave us
    they.   breathe ever
   in our ideals

  never.   disappointing
  never.   breaking promises
never.   shifting from our well placed

     memory
  good or bad. unchanged.

   they.   live on.   (ever).
       as a
melding.   of who they were
& what we wished them to be.

53.

my love
what is love
but a choice?
Then
i will choose
you every day
Until eternity
& then begin again.

54.

i remember
the exact moment
i first recognized
his hands
hard & leathered
cracked along the knuckles …the tips
he worked with metal
spent his days fracturing
large sheets of steel
into smaller pieces of steel.   into smaller bits of steel
(but always steel)

i was a child
who sat
at the opposite
end of the table
cross legged
with my small hands
in front of me
i would
watch him
eat milk poured over
canned peaches & store bought cake
with those craggy hands.
they never reached
out to me
in anger
—-never caused me pain
they.
never reached for me at
all

they sought
a cold one
after a hard day
or a remote
on game day
or a tin of snuff
on any other day
he is gone now
& I no longer that child often find myself
at his grave sitting cross legged
my small life in front of me
with the ache
he left behind
—it is odd
the comfort
i gain.
there is more warmth
in soil and sod and sun
than steel.

55.

that. cool day
immersed in vivid orange
& sharper greys
that. cool day
men
bowed down over
Poseidon's afterthought
grasping what little
could be caught
shimmering ethereal forms
birthed in depths
unexplored by sunlight
that. cool day
frigid wind
that wars against
Apollo's demarcation
& thieves
warmth it's solace
finds stone & flesh
unfortified
Odd.
to be here in this place
of barrenness & bounty
—-With you
As the bullfrogs begin to sing.

56.

it.   is no
Shame
to   till   a life
from rocky soil
to   lift & move
& bend.
to   learn
Furrowing
straight lines
are   mythology
…tales told
by every tiller
of   soil
since.   antiquity
roundness
circumference.
—curve & flexibility

this is enough
for sowing and reaping.

57.

today.
my world
feels small
as if
contained
within
the rim
of a teacup...
the enigmatic smile
from a passing stranger
(or)
—your
momentary
Acknowledgement.

58.

their silent meal
Could.   have been
    Should.   have been
Amicable.
Camaraderie
over appetizers.
Age'd quiet
brined & salted
….Ripening.

their countenance
Could.   have worn
    Should.   have worn
Satisfaction.
Consolidation
at dessert course.
Sweeten'd company
Sugared & balanced
…Nuanced.

at meals end…
(sans aperitif)

they parted.
Still Hungry.

59.

she.
wove words
that had wounded her
into a blanket
she.
took it outside
spread it generously with pillows
& watched the moonrise

60.

with-him
There.
was always
a flurry
of activity
Questions
& unanswered
to do lists.
(Today)
as she
Grieved
the loss
of everyday love
she settled
into her
thoughts
....new
Unaccustomed to
Use
& found solace
In.   the heat on her hands

In.   the steam rising from
a morning coffee.

61.

i planted the garden today
you'd be
glad to know
there are
Tomatoes
i added rows.
there's green beans   too.
Kentucky Runners.
Potatoes.   concern me
(You always said they were Finicky)
still,   there's a place for them
as well.
time & sun will tell what
Grows.

you. told me Tilling isn't easy.

& Soil upturned still
brings up sobs
so much left there
in the sod

seeds unplanted

left undone
you aren't here
to help harvest what will come.

62.

yes,
go into the world
wide eyed
allow naivety
to guide you
do not surrender
to the notion
that experience is
a more worthy companion
than wonder.
pain will come
(it always comes)
whether
you are jaded or joyous
better to greet it
with an open heart
table laid, food prepared
than allow it to find
you weak and wary
in the narrow room
where you've hidden
yourself away

63.

       she. ran her
            fingers lightly
along a stone wall
     Surprised
           to see
them bleed from the friction
     she.
      held them up
       ragged at the tips
        & watched the sky
go from grey to green
           between them
this. soft ache
  on torn flesh
          made the
clouds feel bigger
she.   closed her fists
  thrust hands
    in pocket
     & accepted this pain
as part of her.

home.

64.

i. do not know
the way home...
the path was lost in finding footing
&
i cannot reconcile true north
lost is the warmth of early morning
Sunlight
exchanged for the
Shadows
of afternoons slipping into nightfall
how can i find my way back.
to understanding
wooden.   floors &
rocking chairs
& hollowed out corners.   filled
with. softness.
i.   have lived   like a wild thing
Caved
Hunted
convinced i was.   hunted
duvet covers.   pillow shams.
& kind words
only...remind me... of moments
when. there. weren't. any.
perhaps now that
Sparseness
has entered my soul
there isn't room
for.   plenty.

65.

my love
i have never considered
the moon
a harbinger of gods
i looked instead
to stars....
peered at velvet night
celestial   tapestry dotted
in ever folding
infinities...
longing to touch
what lay just beyond
my breath. my breadth.
my reach...
to run my fingers through
galaxies nourished
by ancient cosmic loam
of a thousand
fiercer lights
of a million lesser homes
my love
can i—finite creature that
i am
broken. terrestrial.
unbound...
(from the first soul)
reclaim those distant
points of fractured
suns that once
adorned your gaze
return the universe to
divinity
& to you.

66.

& in moments
where
words fail us
i will.
capture their
un-uttered syllables
with soft lips
turned inward
from the weariness of
the world.

67.

i   slept
in the

spare room
the.   one that had mattress
upon mattress stacked
so high.
i
could almost brush away
cobwebs in the corner of the ceiling
with my fingertips
goodnights smelled like
rose water and nicotine
i.   have never slept so well
Or

wakened with so much light
as i did there
a little girl
birdsong & bacon
specks of dust dancing in
early streams of sunrise.

68.

I woke up
With the scent
Of you
Lingering
On my soul
Whispering
To my heart
Whatever
That moment was
It was love.

69.

      the last of leaves....
    silent retreat of summer
      Athenian offering.
        momentary warmth
   brilliant zirconia promise
      of everlasting sunlit days.
bloom. heedless of death.
       fruit.   too heavy
  for life or reproduction
 bent and bowing (politely)
  over sod hardened in lack
...too few rains ...too thick with roots
tiny anchors of grass holding firm
    scattered spring's delicate
        hope...
    this.   cloudless sky
this.   murmur of last crickets
 this.   peach just past ripeness
  as i.   fall let me tumble
     end over end.
   from warmth.   & brightness
     & chlorophyll
   into   silent evening
      bright with
  stars. set.   Deep.
    in a late
   September sky

70.

she sat with him,
afternoon sun
spilling on their shoulders
glinting beads of sweat
trailing across her
clavicle
listening…to the symphony
of
whispering insects
singing ballads
tales of nectar'd honeycomb
to swaying grass
&   wild. coneflower.
they sat.
words with him,
not necessary here
emotion instead- spilling.
his eyes to hers
expressed- in small.   pauses.
returned.   glances.

she listened...
to this orchestral sound
of passion expressed in
fluted pitches
& woods
& woodwinds
what.   they knew
what.   was known
lingered on the tongue
like the fading
trajectory of the sun
all at once perceived
& unfathomable
painted. in
the colors
of an indescribable sunset.

71.

do. not.
promise me tomorrow
debt laden promises on
un-banked minutes

you cannot spend
what you

do. not.　　have

(instead)
hold my hand.
say nothing.

& in that small　gesture
i will invest my life.

72.

I know who I am, little girl
I know who I am
I have endured the lion & ascended mountain
I know who I am, know who I am

I know where my feet are headed, little girl
I know what drives them
I have walked the miles & turn my aged-soul to the horizon
I know who I am, know who I am

I am not afraid of your ridicule
I do not fear your need
to see me as a fading light.
the lantern cracks, the fire burns bright.

I know what I know, little girl
I know what I know
the lies of youth I've overcome them
I know who I am, know who I am.

73.

        your.   presence
             is. felt.
in.   stippled skin along my
      neck. pressed.
        Caressed…
         almost.
un-needed…these light
     echos of your
       Cadenced
      steps toward
   my.   soul.
   (rhythms set to
a metronome of hearts
       & breath)
         no.
  your.   soul arrives
     so loudly
it.   need not be
   announced.

74.

i don't need you.
i want you.
& why you cannot see
that (That)
is the better part
i cannot comprehend
i need to breathe
i want to live breathlessly
i need to eat
i want to taste deliciously
everything making this
life so beautiful is
wrapped up in the wanting
(not the needing)
why would i shackle
your independence or
mine to something
as routine & biological
as need?
darling. i want you.

trust me...
(That)
is the better part.

75.

i am waiting for.
a.   storm at sea
a. perfunctorily. stated sentence
a day without clouds
i am waiting for
a whispered conversation
a thrum of tympani
a. sigh.   in the laughter
i am   waiting.   for a moment
i. am waiting for
a. figure at the tree line
a   perched bird
a syllable
i am waiting for
a shift in my given name
a taste of vine. ripened. sweetness.
a brush of fingertips
i am waiting for
a chance to lose
a.   deep. throbbing ache
a question to answer
i am waiting for

76.

i planted a promise for you today.
buried it deep in loamy earth
it
was a small wish
seeded with the soul of a baobab

77.

summer evening.   years ago.
a lingering taste
rich; rolling off the tongue.
in greens. & dreams & pinto beans
haze. & blue forget
me not
i (little me) watch mosquitoes
circling the dampness
near the cover of the spring well
Listen.
to the sound of laughter
coming in waves
from the wooden porch
& lawn chairs. the old kind
that burn your behind
at the end of a hot day.
Somebody.
takes out a beat up guitar.
starts to play
strums
that song.
(everybody knows that one)
& she hums
while she rocks& snaps beans
and lights dim
stars offer better light then
peering through a humid
twilight
curtain

when i get lost.   (and i often do)
i remember that sound…
cicadas.
& her low. rumbling. hum.
the one
that.   started in her soul
found it's way in reverberations
to the back of her lips.

& i remember the path home.

78.

let's fall in love
...Slowly
Tea. tastes best
Steeped low...

taking time
to simmer
as aromatic leaves
bestow

lingering greens
chrysanthemum
dancing on your lips
then tongue
& dark & sharp & warm & clove

too much heat
breeds bitter
boiling passions
spoil the sweet

want burns longer
at an ember
Please-slowly-
fall in love with me.

79.

amazing how
well emptiness
fills
the room
settles.
into
recesses & cracks
along drywall
...baseboards
(my soul)
all the places
warmth
& afternoon sun
used to know
embers.
undo
brilliance & syncope
leaving smoke stains
....shadows
(memory)
surrendered now
to vast moments
without
you.

80.

dim red tail lights
through the fog
& windshield condensation
the defrost
never works right
on nights
like tonight.
….Starless
soaking in, coloring in
shades of ink met sky
light & the slight shimmer of tears
the hum of
tires &
static of one radio station
sort of coming through.
miles to go
miles unanswered
between me & you.

81.

Did I exist before
You?
Did I breathe?
I don't recall breathing...
It's As if upon our
First meeting
My lungs discovered
Air.
Relinquished their
Embryonic idea
Of light and life
For this co-mingling
Of oxygen
Nitrogen
Water vapor
You.

82.

I know
You feel it
Too
My pulling away
Distancing
Myself from
You
It isn't what you think
I'm distancing
From me
From the bile
In the back of my
Throat when I
Watch you
Lay beside me
Knowing
I have given you
More than I
Should
Wrapped my
Universe
In the spaces
Between your
Breath

83.

Dawn whispered,
come with me
& I   powerless
To resist her
Washed myself
in the mystery
of an unsung
day hidden in her
Pale
rose robes.

84.

i'm blinded by tears
at random moments
-when I'm making an omelet
-or washing a duvet cover
sobs so hard
i have to sit down.
he left.
i am searching for scraps of him
pieces of a
hand i never held
reaching for the comfort
of old words scribbled
aimlessly on
envelopes as we talked.
voice-notes
played & replayed
just.   to hear their sound.
he left.
-this time feels less like 'needs time'
- more like the 'it's the last time'.
i try to comfort. myself.
use phrases like
i tried my best.
&. you always talk too much anyway
& you knew he wouldn't stay.
he left.

was all that i had offered
of my.   heart
just another
burden to
Carry?

85.

build me a mansion
my love
elaborate gilded columns
etched ornate with pomegranate
early glances
& parking lot kisses

construct me a manor
my dove
lush velveted gardens
festooned with vine & tiger lily
maddening mornings
& nocturnal blisses

for we two are rich
beyond
measure of gold
for we two hold deed to
this love
that.
we own.

perhaps it be a castle
be-loved
woven tapestry'd walls
rooms full of ancient glazed
paintings
(Or something
more humble)
i'll count my self wealthy
at the sum of love this is.

86.

     there.   was always love
    -even when dingy paneling
  along the basement stairs warped
       from. condensation.
-even. when fabric pulled from the roof
   of that brown. Buick.   you thought

   made you look sophisticated
  -even. when you used to take
        (mouthfuls)
  of the pink and white pain pills
   i cannot recall the name of
     there. was always love

    there.   was always anger
    -even. during drives to
    all you can eat buffets
   on sunlit. back county roads
-even when we watched. your favorite
      black & white tv
 shows curled up contentedly
    among.   pillows on the couch
-even when skies were tinged
    with oranges & ambers
  there.   was always (always). anger

  perhaps if we had found a way
     to. reconcile the.   two.
    there.   would be more
         than
   space & sod between us.

87.

maybe.   this is how
things wash away
to sea
from. shore
Not.
all at once
but rather   bit by bit
steady waves
dislodging them
from sand
ribbons of saltwater
encircling.   drawing them
until they
are pulled back into
the depths
by time
& constancy
(as if they were never there)

88.

                & there you stand
                    backlit.
          by a thousand star fires
          your   gaze. intense.
   fuse atoms   materialize substance
           & carbon & moments
        (that make my heart race)
          You. all of you
            formed. whole.
            celestial enough
   a.   gravitational pull
    creating your own galaxy…
    forged in ancient solitude
        unrested upon.   victory

                & me
    this lost bit of moon dust
     drawn in to circle   you
  your brilliant light. your dark matter.
              until this
    & all that existed before us
             fades into
             Oblivion.

            (Supernova)

89.

there is a barren
sparseness
on January, early,
when leaves refuse
To gather
on the currents
of south wind
& warmth
is driven from new sun
by snowdrops, lingering,
A frozen
Stillness
Permeates.
dawn air, blue sky, my soul...
It Whispers tales of
Spring regained
To a child of hoary cold.
I will take my barrenness
& walk the ice back home

90.

      some are
    Birthed. to knowledge
to unraveled atoms and twine
 to gears & words & windmills
     to solutions
        pronged and tined

      some are
   borne.   to finding
in discovered mirth and quiet hopes
to clear smiles & dreams.   fulfilled
 to goodwill won ….like trophies

       some
   conceived. to fire
in cindered ash & raging flame
to chaos, myth   and passion
  a Gemini to tinder'd pain

    & some are
  met. to loss.   and storm
a sea swept love child of the two
 (perhaps) that is the heart I share
  with such a soul. as you.

91.

what.   role do you play?
who.
are you to me?
to.   my world?

(tell me dearest....)
how do you define
the role.   of gravity?

i mean.
we know
what it does...
but what is it? exactly?

there is no.
comprehending
a.   world without it
even in moments
when we.
(in our advancements...)
leave.
gravity.
float.
aimlessly.

we   only understand
weightlessness
because our feet
have walked.   rooted
on terra firma

& (that.)
is your role
your. very. existence.
defines
everything.

92.

i think.
i might.
be in love
(if it is a place)
i'm unsure.
as I have.
never been (here) before
well…
except.   as
a tourist
(in line)
with
other tourists
Behind…
a velvet rope.

i think.
i might.
be in love
(if it is possible)
to have.
stumbled.
foot first (into)
an
ancient temple

i'm not.
Nor.
(have ever been)
a demigod
so.
i do not know
what
arrow laid
to Cupid's bow
(may) sting like
Nonetheless.
love.   would appear
to be (at minimum)
imminent
at least
that's what.
my heart has whispered to me.
(as untrustworthy a source)
as
that may be.

93.

i. have loved you in autumn
slowly stripped bare
of all urgency
& heat
i have loved you
in passionless
resignation
at the last call of geese
austere skies.   un-idealized.
i have.   I am.
loving you in this process of
dying.
leaving.   a surrender to falling.
trees relinquishing hue
earth rejecting bloom.
i have loved you
in. moments. before.   the prologue
every chapter, writ season…
this unhurried.   ending
i have loved
you raging.   in storm
in subtleties.   unformed.
in
deludes & delusions
impressions
& occlusions

i. have not.   loved
you evergreen.
i am not.   evergreen
not once.
i have loved you.
in burnt oranges & siennas
ochres…too…
an imperfect placing of color
an impression of vividly
tangibly . this is what i offer…
the measure
the method
of all that was
cricket & moon-glow
tumbling. undone…
ever
in fading
finalities
i have loved you.

94.

i. will remember you
to the stars.   tonight
softly laugh with them
over peppermint tea & the shared.
odds & ends.   of memory
your.   smile... at twilight
how you wove
grass between your fingers as we
discussed dinosaurs & how to chop vegetables & the.   universe.
remind myself
&.   the northern light
how it sounded.
just us two.
footsteps.   on gravel road.
accompanied.   by moon
i. will remember you.
to the stars.   tonight
reminisce.   about
the.   softness of your lips
pressed gently.   to my own
that first time i ever felt.   at. home.
was with your breath.   on mine
mingled like the darkness
between stars. more.   beyond
that first impression. unending celestial
boundaries.

```
            your voice.        in my ear
            your voice.        in my soul.
                i.  will.  remember you
               to the stars.... tonight
                    sitting.   wrapped.
                   in the softest blanket
                              i.  can find
              holding my knees & remembering
your warmth       with those luminous gods who
                     knew us both.
                     staying.   there.
                until the cold air.      runs red
          along the tip of my nose…. my cheeks…
                    permeates my legs
                           from
          the.        October ground
                         beneath.
```

95.

tomorrow.
it's soon enough.
to worry about
what.   to call this.
what.   Name to assign
to dappled undulating
sunlight.   through leaves
what.   to call the warmth of you
the.   melody of your voice
the.   sweetness of your lips
tomorrow…
we shall take pen to paper
and chart a future
if.   you care to.
(though I am certain
Enough)
today.   let me bask
in surrendered flesh
name it love
in
hushed & holy tones.

96.

i.   am emptied of the need
to.   understand eternity
freed.   from moorings
this hierarchy of.   attraction…
the magnetic   pull of sky
& the   endless   voluminous
waves.   that dictate.   reality…
i.   am.   content.
with.   present.   tense
drawn instead to momentary pleasures
that.   taste like cocoa butter
on.   my tongue
{these}.   trappings of
a hermit
Terran possessions
carried in flesh   since.   i too am flesh.
bound. together with
-string
-frayed
its spindled threads.   pre-dating
the understanding
measurement of breath.
& it's relationship to
the afternoon sun's
warmth on our bared skin
…even in the cold of October.

97.

        to love.   this man
    is. to love. a lonely night
starless solitude.   an uncertain dawn
  then…risen warmth & sweetness
        to.   love him
        is. to love
          lingering rare
        moments
   not. daily doses
      he is ever
endless boundaries redefined
  ceaseless exploration
    sudden affections
this. this. is what it will mean
    to.   love him

    to.   love this man
   is.   to live. secure in
satisfaction. there will be nothing
   & there is everything
neither of the two can be bidden
     it is duality
  it.   is.   singularity.

he. will never
be constrained in social niceties
he will return, and he will leave
always. (always). loving you
this. is his kindest truth.
should. you choose
to love him too.

to love.   this man.
is to stand
ever present
at.   the horizon line binding chaos & bliss
there is no safety loving him
he will wound. unintentionally.

to love this man.
is to learn. the strength
of your softness
& kept honey'd femininity
a lioness's ferocity.
to advance. surrender.
refuse defeat.
to embrace your own.   company.

to.   love this man
is.   to love yourself
he will accept no less give no more
& in it you will
both be found complete.

98.

Simple promise
momentarily
fermenting in my memory
& summertime
&summertime
water.　　from a garden hose
filling up　　a plastic pool
Someone's making breakfast
it smells divine
maple'd sweetness
　　　　& something fried
She
in a tank top
hair pulled high
gathering dandelions
to make dandelion wine.

99.

      when i leave
    this life   love
             do not
   place   me
  in the ground
vaulted   & secured
          as a repository
  for flowers
      & grief
  Instead.
  reduce   a life
   well loved to ash
  & Scatter me
on willful autumn winds
        so that
   (Perhaps)
          on gray days
the warmth of who i was
    can dance around you
   the way i did
on   pancake'd sunlit
  Saturday
mornings with socks on.

100.

i have always found the term
'darling'
misplaced. uneasy.
it didn't just roll
from   the tip of my tongue.

it.   made no sense
to.   my heart

however.   upon knowing you

i have found it's definition
hidden in the warm folds
of your jacket
traced upon the back of your palms
lingering in the depths of your
countenance.

i want.   to whisper
'welcome home my darling'

welcome.   home.
my love.